IN THE FLOYD ARCHIVES

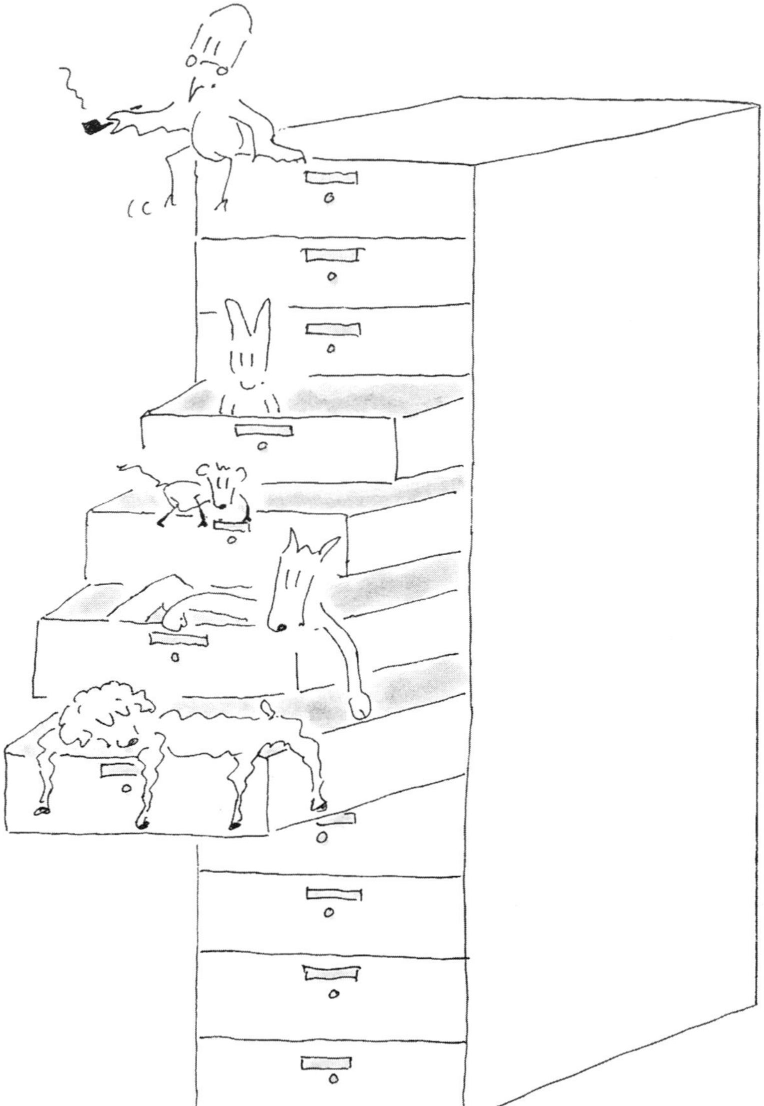

IN THE FLOYD ARCHIVES

A PSYCHO-BESTIARY

SARAH BOXER

Pantheon Books, New York

 Published in the United States by Pantheon Books, a division of Random House, Inc., New York, and simultaneously in Canada by Random House of Canada Limited, Toronto.

Pantheon Books and colophon are registered trademarks of Random House, Inc.

Library of Congress Cataloging-in-Publication Data

Boxer, Sarah.
In the Floyd archives : a psycho-bestiary/Sarah Boxer.
p. cm.
ISBN 0-375-71442-1
1. Psychoanalysis—Comic books, strips, etc. I. Title.
PN6727.B685 I52 2001 741.5′973—dc21 2001021051

www.pantheonbooks.com

Book design by M. Kristen Bearse

Printed in the United States of America
First Edition
2 4 6 8 9 7 5 3 1

For my parents
Florine & Phillip

FLOYD IS NOT FREUD

The Floydian case histories, despite their striking similarity to the Freudian case histories, are a world apart.

I was led into the Floydian world by Mr. Bunnyman. I have drawn this rabbit for as long as I can remember, and he has always looked a little troubled to me. But it was not until a few years ago that I thought to myself, "Why not put Mr. Bunnyman in psychoanalysis and see if his burdens can be lightened?"

So I called in Dr. Floyd—a psychoanalytic bird, and a flighty one at that. Dr. Floyd is more Freudian than Freud, willing to build an interpretation on the slimmest evidence.

When Mr. Bunnyman tells Dr. Floyd that he is being chased by a wolf, Dr. Floyd thinks that the wolf is a paranoid fantasy brought on by Mr. Bunnyman's attachment to his mother. Freud made a similar diagnosis in the case of Little Hans, who feared horses and their giant "widdlers." As Floyd soon discovered, Mr. Bunnyman, like Freud's patient Little Hans, also feared other large animals and confused dung—or, as Hans put it, "lumfs"—with babies.

But there is a wolf at the door, and he decides to stay for his own treatment. Like Freud's Wolf Man, Mr. Wolfman is a bit of a bully. He calls his analyst a swindler and brags that he likes torturing small animals. But he also has a soft side that he does not share with everyone. He is a wolf in sheep's clothing.

Lambskin, Mr. Wolfman's alter ego, demands her own analysis. In the Floydian case histories, Lambskin has a lot of historical, and hysterical, weight to bear. Alternately sullen and giddy, limp and animated, she shares many features with Freud's most famous hysteric. Like Dora, whose father offered her up to his friend so he could carry on an affair with the friend's wife, Lambskin was thrown to the wolves at an early age.

That leaves one character, Ratma'am. She is a rare creature in the psychoanalytic literature, a nonhysterical female. But Ratma'am, a pack rat, is plagued by plenty of other problems. Like Freud's Rat Man, she is anally fixated, obsessive, and wracked with guilt over a pair of eyeglasses. She also has a washing compulsion. But can her worries be entirely neurotic? After all, she is a rat—a filthy creature who leaves droppings everywhere.

Dr. Floyd has a full caseload. Can the problems of four mixed-up mammals be solved by a bird? Or will their stories drive the avian analyst crazy? The answer is in the Floyd Archives.

THE SMOKING PIPES

Freud once said, "Sometimes a cigar is just a cigar." But that is not Floyd's philosophy. In his world, a pipe is never just a pipe. In the following pages, a smoking pipe dropped into the cartoon frame signals a Freudian parallel. You can ignore the smoking pipes or follow them to their Freudian sources in the notes, beginning on page 129.

DR. FLOYD

DR. FLOYD
DR. FLOYD
DR. FLOYD
HELP ME, DR. FLOYD!
THIS WAY TO THE COUCH, MR. BUNNYMAN.
I DON'T NEED THE COUCH. I'M JUST HIDING.
AREN'T WE ALL?
NO, I REALLY AM HIDING. SEE?
WHAT ARE YOU HIDING FROM? COME OUT AND TELL ME.
I'M BEING CHASED BY A WOLF.

SO, YOU THINK YOU'RE BEING "CHASED"?
YES, I AM AFRAID OF THE WOLF.
AND I SUPPOSE THIS "WOLF" WANTS TO EAT YOU UP.
THAT'S RIGHT! HOW DID YOU KNOW?
PERSECUTION FANTASIES ARE COMMON FOR BUNNIES.
BUT I SAW HIM!
THAT'S WHAT THEY ALL SAY.
? ? ?
WE'RE OUT OF TIME. BUT I'LL HOLD THIS SPOT FOR YOU.
YOU SAVED MY LIFE!
I'M GLAD YOU HAD THE SENSE TO SEEK HELP.
COME IN, MR. WOLF-MAN.
DR. FLOYD

WHAT'S THE PROBLEM, MR. WOLFMAN?
I'M ALL TIED UP IN KNOTS.
I HAVEN'T KILLED A THING IN DAYS!
SO WHAT?
I OUGHT TO KILL YOU, YOU DIRTY SWINDLER!
WE'RE HERE TO TALK ABOUT OUR FEELINGS— NOT ACT THEM OUT!
I CAN'T HELP IT. AFTER ALL, I'M A WOLF.
WHEW!
BUT SOMETIMES I WONDER IF I AM A WOLF DEEP INSIDE...

THEN WHAT DO YOU THINK YOU ARE?
MY DAD USED TO DRESS ME UP IN A LAMB-SKIN.
ZIP ME UP, DADDY!
AND I MUST ADMIT, I KIND OF LIKED IT.
PERVERT!
HE ASKED FOR IT!
POOR KID!
FATHER WOULD CHASE ME AND THROW ME OVER HIS SHOULDER LIKE A PIECE OF MEAT.
DIDN'T THAT SCARE YOU?
WELL, YES, BUT IT WAS SO EXCITING.
TIME'S UP.

HOW DID YOU GET IN?
I SLIPPED THROUGH THE CRACKS.
CAN I HELP YOU?
I CERTAINLY HOPE SO.
WHAT'S IN THE BAG?
MY LOOT.
I AM A THIEF, DR. FLOYD. CAN YOU HELP ME?
TELL ME WHATEVER POPS INTO YOUR HEAD.
CRUMMY LIFE, CRUMMY LIFE.
YOU DON'T MIND IF I SNACK, DO YOU?

I THINK I'M GETTING THE HANG OF THIS FREE ASSOCIATION THING.
CRUMBS!
I KNOW... I GET IT... CRUMMY LIFE... CRUMBS... SO WHAT?
LET'S TALK ABOUT YOUR BAG OF CRUMBS.
TO BE PERFECTLY HONEST, SOMETIMES I GET CONFUSED.
I CAN'T TELL WHERE MY BAG ENDS AND I BEGIN.
SO, YOU THINK YOU ARE JUST YOUR BAG?
DON'T BE SILLY, DR. FLOYD...
...I HAVE A LOT MORE THAT'S BURIED!

WHO WAS THAT WOLF AT YOUR DOOR?
WHAT WOLF?
DON'T PLAY DUMB. I SAW HIM WITH MY OWN EYES.
I THINK HE FOLLOWED ME AGAIN TODAY.
DO I NEED TO REMIND YOU ABOUT PARANOIA AMONG BUNNIES?
! ! !
DO I NEED TO REMIND YOU THAT MY MOTHER WAS KILLED BY A WOLF?
GOOD! GOOD! ANGER IS GOOD!
SO, YOU WISH YOUR MOTHER HAD BEEN KILLED BY A WOLF!

WHAT ARE YOU SAYING?
THAT MY MOTHER WAS NOT KILLED BY A WOLF?
WHAT MAKES YOU THINK SHE WAS?
THAT'S WHAT MY BROTHERS AND SISTERS SAID...
...WHEN MOM DIDN'T COME HOME.
ISN'T IT POSSIBLE THAT SOMETHING ELSE HAPPENED?
MY MOTHER DID NOT ABANDON ME!
DID I SAY THAT?
LOOK, I JUST CAME HERE TO HIDE FROM THE WOLF.
AND HERE YOU ARE TALKING ABOUT YOUR MOTHER... HMM.
I WANT YOU TO STARE DOWN THAT "WOLF" AND DISCOVER YOUR REAL FEAR.

DR. FLOYD
YOU MAY COME IN NOW... UH... UH... I DIDN'T CATCH YOUR NAME.
MY, MY, DR. FLOYD! WHAT A SHORT MEMORY! YOU REMEMBER MR. WOLFMAN? WELL, I GOBBLED HIM UP!
MR. WOLF-MAN? IS THAT YOU?
CAN YOU HEAR ME BETTER NOW, DR. FLOYD?
MUCH BETTER! BUT WHICH ONE OF YOU WILL BE TALKING?
BOTH OF US! CAN'T YOU SEE? WE'RE INSEPARABLE.
O.K., BUT I CHARGE SEPARATELY FOR EACH OF YOUR MULTIPLE PERSONALITIES.
LET ME GO FIRST!
THAT'S WHY I BROUGHT YOU, LAMBSKIN.

EVERYONE THINKS I'M SWEET BECAUSE I'M A LAMB.
YOU'RE A LAMBSKIN DEAR, NOT A LAMB... REMEMBER?
ISN'T SHE SWEET?
HE INSISTS ON CALLING ME "LAMBSKIN." IT'S SO DEMEANING.
BUT THAT'S WHAT YOU ARE.
I HAVE A FEELING THAT I'M NOT.
YOU SEE WHAT I HAVE TO CONTEND WITH? SHE THINKS SHE IS SOMEBODY!
WHO WERE YOU JUST TALKING TO?
I WAS JUST TRYING TO HUMOR HER.
HUMOR HER? WHO?
MY LITTLE LAMBSKIN!
LET ME INTERRUPT HERE.
I THINK I'D BETTER SEE YOU ALONE NEXT TIME.
SEPARATION ANXIETY!

YOU'RE EARLY, RAT-MA'AM.
YUP.
AND I SEE YOU'VE BROUGHT YOUR BAG AGAIN.
YES, I PLAN TO SNACK.
EVERY-THING IN HERE IS STOLEN, YOU KNOW.
I GO THROUGH EVERYONE'S GARBAGE AND TAKE WHAT I WANT.
NOW I'M HERE TO UNBURDEN MYSELF.
PLEASE, NO CRUMBS.
I HAVE EVEN STOLEN FROM YOU.
I BET YOU'RE DYING TO KNOW WHAT I TOOK FROM YOU.
I'M DYING TO KNOW WHY YOU'RE TRASHING MY OFFICE.

I'M READY TO BE PUNISHED.
I'M READY TO TELL YOU WHAT I STOLE.
MY POOR COUCH!
NO! NO! MUCH SMALLER THAN A COUCH! GUESS AGAIN.
CRUMBS!
NO! BIGGER THAN CRUMBS.
MY GOD! YOU'RE TERRIBLE AT THIS.
CAN'T YOU THINK OF ANYTHING ELSE?
MY COUCH!
WHY ARE YOU LEAVING CRUMBS ON MY COUCH?
I FEEL THAT I'VE TAKEN SO MUCH FROM YOU...
IT'S TIME FOR ME TO GIVE SOMETHING IN RETURN.

WEEK THREE ANXIETY

DR. FLOYD, YOU WERE RIGHT ABOUT THE WOLF.
YOU DOUBTED ME?
YES, WHEN I SAW THE WOLF AT YOUR DOOR.
LET'S TALK ABOUT IT.
I FINALLY DECIDED TO STOP RUNNING FROM MY FEAR.
AND IT WASN'T A WOLF AT ALL! IT WAS SOMETHING MUCH SOFTER!
A LAMB?
BAAH!
HELLO.
HOW DID YOU KNOW?

TELL ME ALL ABOUT IT.
I WAS ENCHANTED.
MY HEART WAS POUNDING!
BUT BEFORE I COULD EVEN SPEAK, SHE SKIPPED OFF.
SO, YOUR REAL FEAR ISN'T THE WOLF, BUT THE ENCHANTING CREATURE WHO SKIPPED OFF BEFORE YOU COULD SPEAK.
WHAT DO YOU MEAN?
YOUR MOTHER.
MY MOTHER IS DEAD.
IS SHE?

I GOT RID OF THAT SILLY LAMBSKIN, JUST LIKE YOU SAID.
I DIDN'T TELL YOU TO DUMP HER. I JUST SAID I WANTED TO SEE YOU ALONE.
ANYWAY, I FEEL LIKE A REAL WOLF NOW THAT I'VE DITCHED HER.
BUT I THOUGHT YOU LOVED DRESSING UP AS A LAMB.
NO, MY FATHER DRESSED ME IN LAMB'S CLOTHING TO HIDE MY WOLFISHNESS.
BUT YOU'RE STILL DOING IT.
YOU'RE AFRAID OF MY WOLFISHNESS, JUST LIKE MY DAD WAS.
SORRY, DR. FLOYD!

I CAN'T HELP IT. I JUST LOVE TORMENTING LITTLE CRITTERS
—BIRDS, BUNNIES, TINY HELPLESS INSECTS.
ISN'T THERE ANYTHING THAT TORMENTS YOU?
MY FATHER, MY SISTER, BUTTERFLIES, PICTURES OF WOLVES WALKING UPRIGHT, ...AND...
...AND?
A CERTAIN DREAM...
...A DREAM THAT I WISH I COULD PUSH OUT OF MY HEAD.
NEXT WEEK: THE DREAM.

RATMA'AM, YOUR BAG LOOKS HUGE TODAY.
SO DOES YOUR COUCH!
YOU THINK YOU'RE TOO SMALL FOR MY COUCH...
SO YOU FILL IT UP WITH CRUMBS.
NO. I'M LOOKING FOR THE PRIZE AT THE BOTTOM OF THE BAG.
AND WHAT IS THAT?
YOUR GLASSES, DR. FLOYD.

THIS IS WHAT I STOLE FROM YOU.
THOSE AREN'T MINE. I'M WEARING MY GLASSES, SEE?
BUT YOU HAVE TO TAKE THEM, I CAN'T LIVE WITH THE GUILT.
THEN THROW THEM AWAY. I DON'T WANT THEM.
WHAT?!
IF YOU DON'T TAKE THEM, SOMETHING AWFUL WILL HAPPEN.
I WON'T PLAY.
OH, YOU'LL PLAY. I'LL FIND SOMETHING HERE FOR YOU.
I'LL PAY YOU BACK SOMEHOW!

HOW DID YOU GET HERE?
MR. WOLFMAN DROPPED ME ON YOUR DOORSTEP.
I CAN'T MAKE A MOVE WITHOUT HIM.
AND I KEEP HEARING STRANGE ANIMALS.
MOM? ... MOM?
WHAT A PLUSH BATH MAT!
HELLO, BEAUTIFUL!

LET'S ANALYZE THESE VOICES IN YOUR HEAD.
ONE SOUNDED LIKE A CHILD.
MOM?
DO YOU HAVE KIDS?
NO.
MAYBE THIS VOICE IS YOUR WISH TO HAVE A CHILD.
ONE VOICE WAS HUSKY AND SEDUCTIVE.
AH, THE FANTASY OF LOVE.
THEN A SQUEAKY VOICE VOWED TO ROLL ME LIKE A MAT.
THE MASOCHISTIC WISH — GRANTED.

I HAVE SO MUCH TO TALK ABOUT.
COME LIE DOWN, MR. BUNNYMAN.
I CAN'T STOP THINKING ABOUT THAT CREATURE WHO SKIPPED AWAY.
YOUR MOTHER?
SHE LOOKED LIKE A LAMB TO ME.
AND MY MOM'S DEAD.
BUT CLEARLY YOU CONFUSE THEM.
WELL, ANYWAY, I SAW HER AGAIN.
mom?
I SAW HER LYING ON YOUR DOORSTEP. SHE WAS LIMP.
SHE LOOKED A LITTLE DEAD?

SHE WAS ABSOLUTELY STILL...
...YET I WANTED TO TALK TO HER, TO GET HER ATTENTION.
I BABBLED FOR HOURS ON END...
...WITHOUT GETTING THE SLIGHTEST RESPONSE.
I DON'T KNOW WHAT KEPT ME GOING...
...I WAS JUST DETERMINED NOT TO BE IGNORED.
SO I TALKED AND I TALKED...
...AND THE FUNNY THING WAS...
...I DIDN'T THINK FOR A MOMENT THAT SHE WAS DEAD...
...NO, I STARTED TO THINK THAT I WAS...
...AND THE ONLY THING THAT COULD BRING ME TO LIFE...
...WAS A RESPONSE FROM HER.
BUT AS YOU CAN GUESS, SHE NEVER DID ANSWER.
AND NOW I'M LEFT WONDERING WHETHER I AM ALIVE OR NOT.
DR. FLOYD? DR. FLOYD?!...

ARE YOU STILL HAVING THAT NIGHT-MARE?
YES, I AM LYING IN BED WHEN SUDDENLY THE WINDOW BLOWS OPEN.
I AM TERRIFIED TO SEE A PACK OF WOLVES SITTING IN A TREE, STARING AT ME - ALL SILENT!

TELL ME MORE ABOUT THE WOLVES.
THEY REMIND ME OF THE SHEEP WE USED TO VISIT IN MATING SEASON.
YOU MATED WITH SHEEP?
NO, WE JUST WATCHED.
WHAT ELSE DOES THE DREAM REMIND YOU OF?
A FAIRY TALE.
SOME WOLVES CLIMB A TREE BY CATCHING HOLD OF EACH OTHERS' TAILS,...
CASTRATION ANXIETY!
AND THE LAST ONE GETS HIS TAIL DOCKED.
SNIP!
HEY!

WELL, HAVE YOU FORGIVEN ME YET?
FOR WHAT?
FOR STEALING YOUR GLASSES!
I TOLD YOU, THOSE AREN'T MINE.
WHATEVER. I'VE FOUND SOMETHING ELSE TO GIVE YOU.
CRUMBS AGAIN.
NO. THIS IS MUCH BIGGER.
YOU KNOW THAT I COLLECT TRASH, RIGHT?
YOU CAN IMAGINE HOW DIRTY I GET.
TO KEEP DAINTY I MUST WASH 28 TIMES A DAY.
COMPULSIVE WASHING!

I AM NOT A COMPULSIVE WASHER. I ONLY WASH WHEN I MUST.
BUT 28 TIMES A DAY?!
I AM A RAT, DR. FLOYD. I LIVE IN FILTH.
COME SNIFF ME! DO I SMELL LIKE A COMPULSIVE WASHER TO YOU?
NOW YOU'VE GOTTEN ME WAY OFF MY POINT.
WHICH IS?
THE POINT IS, I NEED A BATHMAT. AND I FOUND ONE.
NICE BATH-MAT!
SOFT 'N WOOLY!
BUT I'M GIVING IT TO YOU AS PAYMENT FOR YOUR GLASSES.

DR. FLOYD
LAMBSKIN! YOU'RE HERE!
WHO BROUGHT YOU HERE TODAY?
ANGELS, ANIMALS. I DON'T KNOW.
I CAN'T MOVE.
SOUNDS LIKE HYSTERIA!
FIRST YOU HEAR STRANGE ANIMALS, NOW YOU'RE A DOORMAT.
WHAT NEXT?
WHAT DO YOU SUGGEST?
HYPNOSIS?
GREAT.

YOU'RE GETTING SLEEPY...
PUT ME UNDER YOUR SPELL, DOC.
SHE'S ALREADY OUT.
I WAS THROWN TO THE WOLVES AT AN EARLY AGE.
WHEN I WAS A KID, THE WOLVES USED TO WATCH OUR FLOCK DURING MATING SEASON.
IT REALLY UNNERVED MY FATHER.
SO HE STRUCK A DEAL WITH THE WOLVES.
IF THE WOLVES WOULD LEAVE US ALONE...
FATHER WOULD PAY A SMALL PRICE...
...ME.

WEEK FIVE

EXPOSURE

IT'S NICE TO SEE YOU, MR. BUNNYMAN.
YOU MEAN YOU CAN SEE ME?
WHY NOT?
I'VE BEEN FEELING INVISIBLE.
...EVER SINCE I TRIED TO GET THAT LAMB'S ATTENTION.
OF COURSE YOU DO. YOUR OWN MOTHER IGNORED YOU.
IT'S NOT JUST HER.
I FEEL LIKE YOU CAN'T SEE ME EITHER.
MR. BUNNYMAN, YOU KNOW I CAN SEE YOU AS LONG AS YOU CAN PAY.
BUT I'M BROKE.

DID YOU HEAR ME?
I CAN'T SEE YOU.
WHAT'S WRONG, DR. FLOYD?! LOOK AT ME.
I CAN'T SEE YOU.
LOOK AT ME! I'M STANDING RIGHT HERE!
I CAN'T SEE YOU.
I MUST BE INVISIBLE.
IN FLOYD WE TRUST
I'VE GOT TO GET SOME MONEY FAST.

MR. WOLFMAN, WHY ARE YOU COVERING YOURSELF?
I FEEL EXPOSED WITHOUT MY LAMBSKIN.
HAVE YOU SEEN HER?
WE'RE HERE TO TALK ABOUT YOU.
LET'S GET BACK TO YOUR DREAM.
AS I SAID... THE WOLVES WERE WHITE —LIKE LAMBSKIN.
DID I TELL YOU HOW WE MET?
THE DREAM, WOLF-MAN.

I ALREADY TOLD YOU MY DREAM, DR. FLOYD.
BUT I HAVE NOT ANALYZED IT YET!
THE TREE REPRESENTS
A MEADOW.
THE WOLVES
...ARE LAMBS.
THEIR SILENCE
... IS GREAT COMMOTION.
I THINK YOU WANT TO SKIP...
LIKE A LAMB.
NO! NO! IT'S NOT TRUE!
I TAKE YOUR PROTEST
... FOR AGREE-MENT.

YOU'RE GONNA LOVE THIS MAT.
YOU'RE GONNA LOVE HOW I ROLLED IT.
IT WASN'T EASY, YOU KNOW.
I HAD TO GET HELP.
AND IT COST ME.
TAP TAP
WHAT ARE YOU TALKING ABOUT?
THE GLASSES.
NOT AGAIN!
I GAVE THE GLASSES TO A BUNNY FOR ROLLING UP THE MAT.
ROLL IT TIGHTER, BUNNY!

THINK ABOUT WHY YOU WANT TO GIVE AWAY THOSE GLASSES.
I'M THINKING ... I'M THINKING!
TOO BIG!
THEY'RE TOO BIG.
NO, SOME-THING ABOUT YOU.
I'M TOO SMALL.
SOME-THING FROM CHILD-HOOD.
I WAS SMALLER THEN.
AND?
THE GLASSES WERE BIGGER.
NO.
SNAP!
I WAS A SNEAKY, SNIVELING LITTLE SPY AS A CHILD.
THAT'S WHAT DAD USED TO SAY.
ARE YOU GONNA SPANK ME?

NOW, WHERE WERE WE?
COULD YOU FINISH UNROLLING ME FIRST?
YOU WERE TELLING ME HOW YOUR DAD THREW YOU TO THE WOLVES.
DID I TELL YOU HOW ONE OF THEM POUNCED ON ME?
WHO? MR. WOLFMAN?
COUGH! COUGH!
IT WAS HORRIBLE. I FELT HIS TAIL THRASHING.
YOUNG LOVE!!
HARDLY, DR. FLOYD.
WHY WOULD A LAMB WANT TO BE MAULED BY A WOLF?
TO GET HER FATHER'S ATTENTION,
TO PUNISH HER MOTHER,
AND TO GIVE IN TO EVERY LAMB'S INNERMOST DESIRE.

COUGH COUGH
DO YOU HAVE A COLD, LAMBSKIN?
NO, JUST A TICKLE.
IT STARTED AFTER...
...AFTER MR. WOLFMAN POUNCED ON ME.
YOUR COUGH IS A SIGN OF EXCITE-MENT.
YOU'RE IN LOVE WITH THE OLD WOLF.
AND YOU CAN'T ADMIT IT.
COUGH! COUGH!
WHAT DID YOU DO WHEN MR. WOLFMAN POUNCED?
I SLAPPED HIM!
HE LOVED IT.

WEEK SIX GUILT

I'M BACK.
AND?
CAN YOU SEE ME?
THAT DEPENDS.
I BROUGHT SOME-THING FOR YOU.
SOME-THING THAT WILL MAKE IT EASIER TO SEE ME.
GLASSES.
TAKE THEM.
I HAVE GLASSES. SEE?
BUT THEY'RE NOT STRONG ENOUGH TO SEE ME.
WHEN YOU SAID YOU COULDN'T SEE ME, I GOT WORRIED.
I WONDERED, WAS I INVISIBLE?
OR WERE YOU BLIND?

SO, I WENT BACK TO THE LAMB TO SEE IF SHE COULD SEE ME.
SHE WAS STILL ON THE GROUND.
A RAT WAS THERE
AND THE RAT WAS TRYING TO FOLD HER UP.
SO, I SAID, "WHADDYA THINK YOU'RE DOING?"
WHO IS THAT?!
YOU CAN'T SEE ME.
THAT'S MY CURSE.
I THINK I'VE GOT THE CURE.
OOH!
GIVE THESE GLASSES TO ANYONE AND THEY'LL SEE YOU.
BUT I CAN'T PAY YOU.
THEN YOU'LL BE MY PORTER.
TIGHTER BUNNY!
YOU ROLLED YOUR MOTHER?!

HELLO, DR. FLOYD.
HELLO.
I'VE BEEN THINKING ABOUT LAMB-SKIN.
STILL?
SHE WAS SUPPOSED TO BE MY PLAYTHING.
BUT SHE BECAME A REAL TEASE.
WHAT?
SHE TAUNTED ME... SHE TEMPTED ME...
AND WHEN I PUT THAT SOFT SKIN ON...
EVERYTHING CHANGED.

TELL ME MORE.
ONCE I GOT INSIDE, SHE WAS QUIET.
IT WAS LIKE I BECAME HER,
ALL SOFT AND WOOLY.
SHORT TAIL.
MY FATHER HAD NO IDEA WHAT HE STARTED.
I WONDER WHAT HE'D DO NOW IF HE SAW ME IN MY LAMBSKIN,
WITHOUT MY LONG TAIL SHOWING.
WOULD HE LOVE ME? OR WOULD HE KILL ME?
ONCE MY DAD CAUGHT ME PLAYING WITH MY TAIL. BOY! WAS HE SORE!
YOU KNOW, LAMBSKIN BARELY HAS A TAIL. SHE NEEDS ME.

HI, DR. FLOYD.
WHERE'S YOUR BAG?
IT WAS TOO MUCH TO BEAR.
GOOD! NOW WE CAN TALK ABOUT EVERYTHING YOU HAVE BURIED.
IT'S ALL VERY HUSH-HUSH.
THE THINGS I HAVE BURIED...
...I HAVE BURIED FOR A REASON.
THEY AREN'T PRETTY
AND THEY AREN'T NICE
BUT THEY ARE MINE
AND I'VE PRESERVED THEM BY BURYING THEM.
AND I'M GOING TO SHARE THEM
WITH YOU NOW.
FOR EXAMPLE, I HAVE... UM...
A PIECE OF GLASS ... GREEN.
AND STRING, AND SEEDS...
WAIT, WAIT, THERE'S MORE.
I HAVE BONES...
AND SHELLS.

AND THEN I ALSO HAVE ...
STOP IT!
WHAT? I THOUGHT YOU WANTED ME TO TALK ABOUT BURIED THINGS.
BURIED THINGS THAT MATTER.
WHY DIDN'T YOU SAY SO?
MY CHILDHOOD
PART ONE
IT ALL STARTED WHEN I WAS YOUNG.
I HAD A CERTAIN REPUTATION.
I LIKED TO PEEK UP SKIRTS
JUST TO SEE WHAT I COULD SEE.
I'M AFRAID WE'RE OUT OF TIME.

HELLO, LAMBSKIN.
DR. FLOYD
ZZZZZ
SHHH! SHE'S ASLEEP.
I WAS DREAMING, DR. FLOYD.
ABOUT WHAT?
A FIRE.
BE A LITTLE MORE SPECIFIC.
MY FATHER WAS TRYING TO SAVE ME FROM A FIRE.
NOW WE'RE GETTING SOMEWHERE.
IT'S YOUR BURNING PASSION.
IT'S HOT WHEN YOU'RE ROLLED UP LIKE A MAT.

DID YOU ESCAPE?
MY MOTHER WOULDN'T LET US LEAVE BEFORE WE FOUND HER JEWEL CASE.
HER JEWEL CASE?! BUT THE HOUSE WAS ON FIRE!
I KNOW.
BUT MY MOTHER LOVES HER JEWEL CASE.
SIGH!
SIGH!
WHAT IS THAT THING YOU'RE FIDDLING WITH?
IT'S A SHELL THAT GOT ROLLED UP WITH ME.
PSST... IT'S A JEWEL CASE.

WEEK SEVEN

ACTING OUT

I'VE BECOME A RAT'S PORTER.
UH-HUH.
SO YOU CAN SEE ME.
IT'S FUNNY HOW THINGS WORK OUT.
HOW DO YOU MEAN?
I CAME TO YOU TO ESCAPE THE WOLF.
AND NOW I'M BEING PAID BY A RAT...
TO HAUL AROUND A LAMBSKIN THAT YOU THINK IS MY MOTHER.
SO, THE WOLF ISN'T BOTHERING YOU ANYMORE.
NOT EXACTLY...
YOU MUST FEEL PRETTY GOOD ABOUT THAT.
I GUESS SO...
DR. FLOYD, THERE'S SOMETHING ELSE.

YOU KNOW MY NEW JOB?
ROLLING UP YOUR MOTHER?
IT MAKES ME A LITTLE NERVOUS.
OH?
SOME-THING FEELS WRONG.
I FEEL LIKE I'M GOING TO BE PUNISHED.
BUT I'VE DONE NOTHING WRONG.
I THINK THE WOLF IS WATCHING ME.
YOUR JEALOUS FATHER?
JUST A THOUGHT.

I HAVE A CONFESSION TO MAKE.
WHAT?
I HAVE BEEN SPYING ON SOME-ONE.
COME LIE DOWN.
I KNOW IT'S VERY BAD OF ME...
BUT IT MAKES ME FEEL GOOD.
I CAN'T HELP IT.
I WORSHIP THE GROUND LAMBSKIN LIES ON.
I KNOW THAT YOU'RE VERY ATTACHED.
I MEAN I LITERALLY WORSHIP THE GROUND SHE LIES ON.
I GO TO HER AND SAY, "LAMB-GOD."

WHAT? WHY?
MAYBE TO PROTECT MYSELF.
FROM WHAT?
FROM BECOMING A LIMP MAT LIKE LAMBSKIN.
HOW LONG HAS THIS BEEN GOING ON?
I'VE ALWAYS BEEN VERY RELIGIOUS. WHEN I SEE DUNG I PRAY.
BUT WORSHIPING LAMBSKIN IS NEW FOR ME.
AND I'M NOT ALONE, DR. FLOYD.
WHAT ARE YOU TALKING ABOUT?
I SAW A RAT PRAYING UNDER HER TAIL.

I'M BACK, DR. FLOYD.
I SEE.
I'M READY FOR PART TWO OF...
MY CHILDHOOD.
WHEN I WAS LITTLE, WE LIVED IN A RATS' NEST.
WE ALL SLEPT IN ONE BIG HEAP.
BUT I ALWAYS MADE SURE I WAS ON TOP.
AS YOU KNOW, I AM A COMFIRMED VOYEUR.
SO I'D ALWAYS REPORT WHAT I SAW.
WHAT'S OUT THERE?
LAMP! TOWEL! PLATE!
BUT ONE DAY, I SAW THE MOST EXQUISITE RAT WALK BY ...AND I TOLD NO ONE.

I STARTED THINKING I COULD WIN HIM OVER...
...IF ONLY MY FAMILY WOULD DIE TRAGICALLY.
THAT WAY THE CUTE RAT WOULD NEVER SEE OUR DIRTY NEST.
AND OF COURSE I'D GET ALL THAT SYMPATHY.
THERE, THERE.
BOO HOO! MY FAMILY'S GONE!
PRETTY SOON I THOUGHT...
I COULD KILL FOR THIS!
BUT THAT'S NOT EVEN THE WORST PART.
THAT'S ENOUGH FOR TODAY!

LET'S GET BACK TO YOUR FIRE DREAM.
RIGHT. MY BURNING PASSION FOR WOLFMAN.
HOW DID YOU FEEL WHEN YOU WOKE UP?
HOT AND BOTHERED.
WERE YOU THINKING OF WOLFMAN?
I THOUGHT I HEARD HIS VOICE.
SO YOU MISS HIM.

DID YOU HEAR ME?
IT'S RIDICULOUS.
HE'S REPULSIVE — A SICK OLD WOLF.
AND YET YOU'RE DYING FOR HIS RETURN.
I AM NOT.
WILL YOU STOP FIDDLING WITH THAT SEASHELL OF YOURS?
YOU KNOW WHAT THEY SAY ABOUT SHELLS?
SSHH HHHH...

WEEK EIGHT CATHARSIS

HOW'S YOUR JOB?
YESTERDAY I WENT TO TALK TO THE LAMB BEFORE ROLLING HER.
BUT THE RAT WAS ALREADY THERE...
UNDER THE LAMB'S TAIL...
LIKE SHE WAS THINKING OF GOING IN...
OR WAITING FOR SOMETHING ...
...TO DROP.
IT REMINDED ME OF SOMETHING.
NATURALLY.
MY MOTHER HAD A LOT OF CHILDREN.
I FEEL KIND OF DEPRESSED.

I WONDERED WHERE WE CAME FROM.
AND?
MY BROTHERS AND SISTERS TOLD ME WE CAME FROM ... YOU KNOW ... LIKE... DUNG.
SO I ASKED THEM, "HOW DOES MOM KNOW THE DIFFERENCE?"
AND THEY SAID
SHE TAKES CARE OF HER KIDS ... THE DUNG SHE LEAVES BEHIND.
THAT WORRIED ME.
I DECIDED TO ASK MOM ABOUT IT OVER BREAKFAST.
BUT THE NEXT DAY WHEN I GOT UP
... SHE WAS GONE.

BLESS YOU, BROTHER FLOYD.
OVER HERE, MR. WOLFMAN.
I VISITED LAMBSKIN AGAIN AFTER I SAW THE RAT PRAYING UNDER HER TAIL.
I DECIDED TO PRAY THERE TOO...
... AND THEN WRAP MYSELF IN THE LAMB...
... FOR SHE IS HOLY.
BUT I THOUGHT...
YOU THOUGHT SHE WAS A PUPPET.
... YOU WERE WORRIED ABOUT BEING LIMP LIKE HER.
I MUST HAVE HER.

ARE YOU IN LOVE?
NO, I JUST MISS THAT SOFT SKIN.
SO WHAT'S STOPPING YOU?
WOLVES WILL PREY ON ME.
THE ONES IN THE DREAM?
NO. IT'S MY FATHER WHO WOULD POUNCE.
HE'D TEAR ME TO PIECES.
AND GOBBLE ME UP!
HE'D LIKE THAT.

I HOPE YOU LIKE THE MAT.
WHY DID YOU GIVE IT UP?
YOU DON'T WANT TO KNOW.
YES, I DO.
NO, YOU DON'T.
IT'S DISGUSTING!
REMEMBER THE DAY I FOUND THE MAT?
NICE BATH-MAT...
SOFT 'N WOOLY
UH-HUH.
WELL, I NEVER TOLD YOU THE NEXT PART.
I STARTED SLIPPING DOWN...
AND I ENDED UP RIGHT UNDER THE TAIL.

SNIFF!
IT WAS QUITE A SIGHT!
IT REMINDED ME OF SOMETHING...
... SOMETHING THAT MY FAMILY CALLED THE "RAT TORTURE."
WHEN I FELL UNDER THAT TAIL
... AN IDEA FLASHED IN MY HEAD...
...IF I DON'T PAY YOU BACK, THEN SOMEONE WILL FACE THE "RAT TORTURE."
I'M CONFUSED.
I CAN'T EXPLAIN NOW. I FEEL DIRTY. I NEED A BATH.
AND I WANT THAT MAT!

STILL COUGHING, LAMBSKIN?
COUGH
I THINK IT'S HYSTERICAL.
YOU SOUND JUST LIKE MY FATHER.
OH? WHAT DOES HE SAY?
HE THINKS I COUGH TO GET ATTENTION.
IT ANNOYS HIM.
COUGH
I KNOW HOW HE FEELS.
DR. FLOYD,... I LOVE MY FATHER ...
I BET SHE LOVES ME, TOO.

I LOVE MY FATHER,
BUT HE IS INSINCERE,
FALSE,
AND SELFISH.
EVEN I AM A BETTER PARENT.
BUT YOU DON'T HAVE KIDS.
I'VE SUCKLED A FEW IN MY DAY...
EVEN WOLF PUPS.
WOLF-MAN'S PUPS?!
WELL, SOMEONE HAD TO DO IT.
THEIR MOTHER WAS ALWAYS -AHEM!-
COUGH
SICK.

WEEK NINE DELUSION

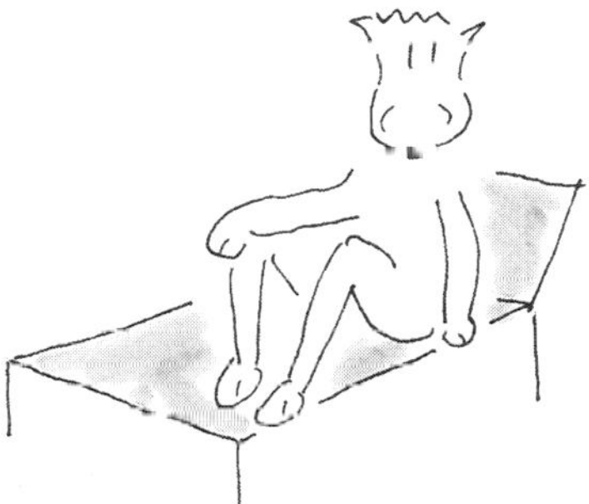

WE STOPPED AT A CRUCIAL MOMENT LAST TIME.
AS I RECALL,
YOU WERE BEING TREATED LIKE CRAP.
I DON'T THINK I SAID THAT.
YOU DIDN'T HAVE TO.
WHAT ABOUT THE WOLF?
AND THE LAMB?
WHY FOCUS ON DUNG?
BECAUSE WE'RE TALKING ABOUT YOU!

I HAVE IMPORTANT DUTIES, YOU KNOW.
ROLLING UP, CARRYING, DROPPING OFF...
WHY DO YOU DO IT?
SO YOU CAN SEE ME.
BUT WHY?
TO GET CLOSER TO YOUR MOTHER?
AND ROLLING HER UP IS THE WAY TO DO IT?
YES.
YES.

ARE YOU CHASING BUNNIES AGAIN?
ME?
JUST WATCHING AND HOLDING MY BREATH.
WHY?
TO PROTECT MY LAMBSKIN.
HOW DOES HOLDING YOUR BREATH HELP HER?
WATCHING IS FOR HER.
HOLDING MY BREATH IS FOR ME.
I HAVE TO HOLD MY BREATH...
OR I MIGHT BECOME WEAK LIKE HER.

BUT DON'T YOU PRAY FOR THAT?
YOU CAN'T REALLY TRUST GOD.
HE'S WRATHFUL AND VINDICTIVE.
I THINK HE'D EVEN KILL HIS OWN SON.
ARE WE TALKING ABOUT GOD OR YOUR FATHER?
GOD-THE-FATHER. HE THINKS I'M HIS PLAYTHING.
RELIGIOUS FEVER!
I AM THE LAMB OF GOD!
GRAND DELUSION!
THAT'S A BIG BUBBLE.
MASOCHISTIC WISHES!

HI, FLOYD.
WE HAVE A LOT TO TALK ABOUT.
YOU NEVER TOLD ME ABOUT YOUR FATHER BEFORE LAST WEEK.
YOU NEVER ASKED.
SO, IF I DON'T ACCEPT SOMETHING FROM YOU, YOUR FATHER WILL SUFFER THE "RAT TORTURE."
RIGHT.
BUT NOT JUST MY DAD.
MY BOYFRIEND IS ALSO IN DEEP DOO-DOO.
WHAT BOYFRIEND?
WHAT FATHER?
WHAT?
MY POINT EXACTLY.

LET'S BACK UP.
IS THIS BETTER?
FIRST, WHAT IS THIS "RAT TORTURE"?
WATCH CARE-FULLY!
FIND A DARK CRAWL SPACE...
AND START SPELUNKING.
VERY DARK!
WHO WILL HAVE TO DO THIS?
FATHER
BOYFRIEND
BUT WHY?
BECAUSE YOU WON'T TAKE YOUR GLASSES.
GOT IT?

THERE YOU GO, LAMBSKIN.
TELL ME ABOUT THE WOLF PUPS.
I NURSED THEM WHEN THEIR MOTHER WAS SICK.
WHICH PROVES THAT YOU WISH YOU WERE THEIR MOTHER.
WHICH PROVES THAT YOU'RE IN LOVE WITH MR. WOLF-MAN.
ISN'T THAT SO?
NO! NO! NO!
"NO" MEANS "YES."
SIGH!

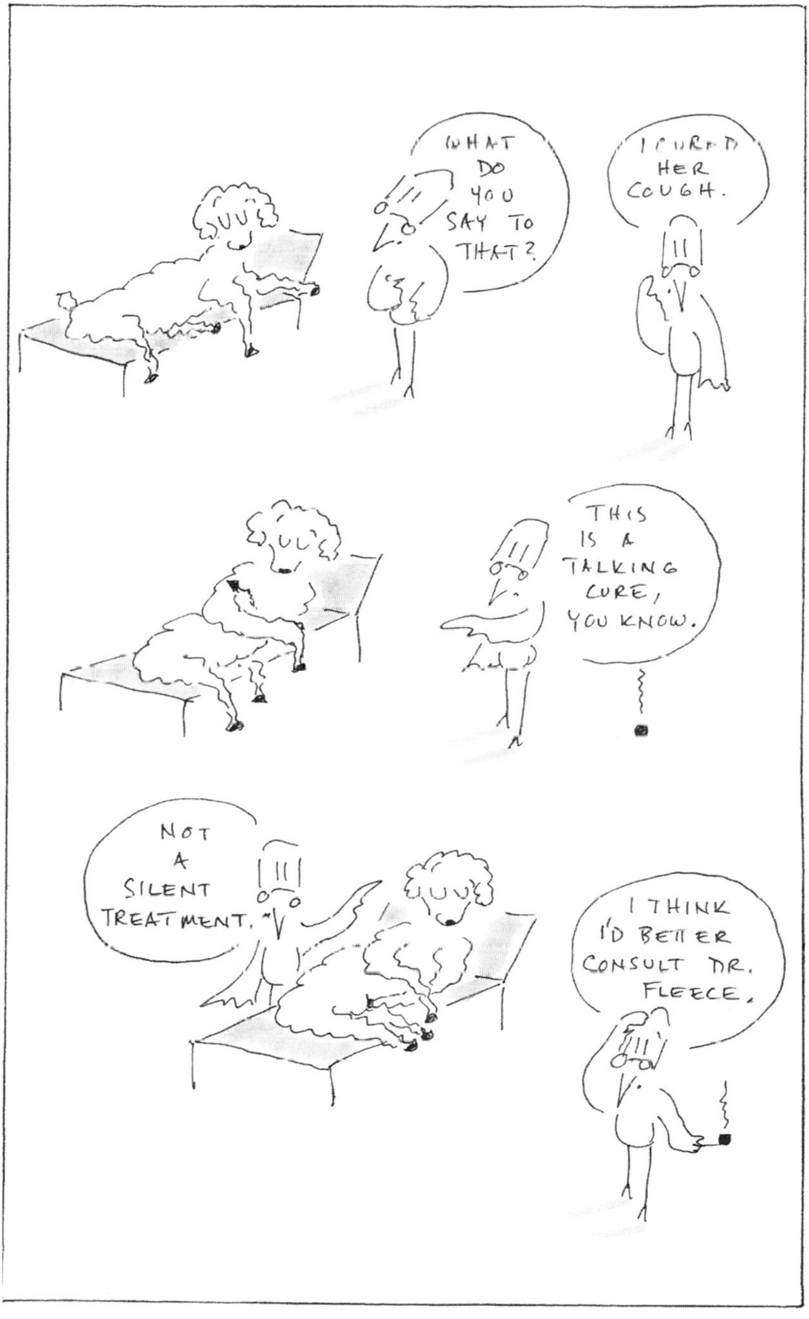
WHAT DO YOU SAY TO THAT?
I CURED HER COUGH.
THIS IS A TALKING CURE, YOU KNOW.
NOT A SILENT TREATMENT.
I THINK I'D BETTER CONSULT DR. FLEECE.

HELLO.
HI.
I HAVE CONDUCTED A TEST.
I CALL IT "LITTLE DUNG OR LITTLE CHILD?"
FIRST I CREEP UP ON HER.
THEN I CRAWL UNDER-NEATH
AS IF I WERE HER CHILD.
IT'S NICE AND WARM THERE.

SO, HOW DID IT GO?
PRETTY GOOD. I WAS TOLERATED.
THEN I CRAWLED UNDER HER TAIL...
...LIKE I WAS... ER...
AND?
I WAS TOLERATED THERE TOO.
WHAT DO YOU CONCLUDE?
I KIND OF PREFER THE IDEA OF STORKS WITH BUNDLES.

I NEED LAMBSKIN BACK.
IT'S PART OF GOD'S PLAN FOR ME.
WHAT ARE YOU TALKING ABOUT?
IN ORDER TO BE THE LAMB OF GOD...
FIRST I MUST BE A LAMB.
WHY?
THEN GOD CAN DO WHAT HE WANTS WITH ME.

I'VE BEEN MEANING TO TALK TO YOU ABOUT THAT.
ABOUT GOD'S PLAN?
NO. ABOUT LAMB-SKIN.
I MUST HAVE HER!
I'M AFRAID THAT'S IMPOSSIBLE.
I HAVE DISCUSSED LAMBSKIN WITH DR. FLEECE.
AND HE HAS AGREED TO PERFORM HIS FAMOUS SURGERY—
THE FLEECING OF THE LAMB!
YOU CAN'T.
SHE'S MINE!
OUR TIME IS UP.

So, where were we?
Oh yes... dreamy beau, ugly home. I could kill my family for this.
But...
I didn't have to. I was out strolling with the rat of my dreams...
And the nest collapsed with my family inside.
Wish fulfilled.
Not exactly. I told the rat everything, including my "wish."
And?
He was disgusted and scurried off.
But what does this have to do with the rat torture?
You've got a mind like a steel trap, Floyd.
It's Oedipal, stupid!

I WENT BACK INTO THE NEST...
I STEPPED CAREFULLY OVER MY DEAD FAMILY...
AND I PACKED EVERY-THING I COULD CARRY...
AND LEFT
FOR GOOD.
EVER SINCE THEN, I'VE FELT A BIT GUILTY. I KILLED MY FAMILY.
DID YOU SAY YOUR FATHER IS DEAD?
YES, DR. FLOYD. FATHER DEAD, ME GUILTY. GOT IT?
NOW I FEEL DIRTY. I NEED A BATH.
YOUR FATHER IS DEAD?
DR. FLOYD, I NEED TO BORROW THE LAMB-SKIN FOR MY BATH.
IF YOUR FATHER IS DEAD, HE CAN'T SUFFER THE "RAT TORTURE."
IT WAS JUST A FANTASY.

I HAVE GREAT NEWS, LAMBSKIN!
DID YOU HEAR ME?
DR. FLEECE HAS AGREED TO FLEECE YOU.
DID YOU HEAR ME?
DR. FLEECE IS A VERY BUSY DOCTOR.
WHAT AN INGRATE!

DON'T YOU WANT TO KNOW WHAT HE WILL DO?
WELL, I'LL TELL YOU.
FLEECE BELIEVES HYSTERIA BEGINS AND ENDS WITH WOOL.
HE'LL SHEAR YOU UNTIL YOU'RE CURED.
SNIP SNIP
!!!
FINALLY, WE'LL SEE WHAT YOU'RE REALLY MADE OF.

WEEK ELEVEN

SLEEPING

HELLO, DR. FLOYD. YOU LOOK WEIRD.
I HAVE SOME NEWS.
I THINK YOU'D BETTER LIE DOWN.
YOUR JOB IS ENDING.
WHAT?
NO MORE ROLLING AND CARRYING THE LAMB.
WHAT?!
FLEECE IS GOING TO HELP HER.
WHO IS FLEECE?
A DOCTOR WITH SCISSORS.

FLEECE BELIEVES ALL TROUBLE BEGINS WITH WOOL.
LAMBSKIN HAS TOO MUCH.
ONCE SHE IS FLEECED, ALL HER TROUBLES WILL VANISH.
SHE MUST BE FLEECED.
WHAT ABOUT ME?
YOU'RE FINE. YOU DON'T NEED TO BE FLEECED.
I MEAN, WILL THE FLEECING HELP HER RECOGNIZE ME?
WELL, THE WOOL WON'T BE OVER HER EYES.

WHERE IS SHE?
WHO?
LAMBSKIN!
YOUR FEMININE SIDE.
WHATEVER. ... WHERE IS SHE?
I'M GETTING HER READY FOR HER FLEECING.
YOUR GIRLISH SIDE HAS GOTTEN OUT OF HAND.
BUT ONCE WE FLEECE LAMBSKIN, YOU'LL BE A REAL WOLF-MAN.

NO MORE LAMBSKIN?
YOU'LL BE ALL WOLF AGAIN.
NO MORE WOLF IN LAMB'S CLOTHING!
NO MORE GIRLY WOLF-MAN.
I'M GONNA BE A WOLF.
LAMBSKIN MUST BE FLEECED.

I SUPPOSE YOU'VE COME TO COLLECT THE MAT.
YOU GOT IT!
I HAVE A PROPOSITION FOR YOU.
I'M LISTENING.
SHALL I GET ON THE COUCH?
YOU HAVE A WASHING COMPULSION...
...BROUGHT ON BY YOUR MURDEROUS FANTASIES.
I'M STILL LISTENING.
THE LAMBSKIN HAS MADE IT WORSE.
WHEN YOU SEE A BATHMAT, YOU WANT TO WASH.
TRUE... TRUE.

SO, I'M HAVING YOUR BATH-MAT FLEECED.
FOR MY SAKE?
DR. FLOYD, YOU SHOULDN'T.
FLEECE HAS ALREADY AGREED TO DO IT.
FOR ME?
HOW WILL I EVER REPAY YOU?
BELIEVE ME, I'VE THOUGHT OF THAT.
YOU'LL TAKE ALL THE WOOL...
AND SRRINKLE IT OVER YOUR FAMILY NEST.
THE SACRIFICIAL LAMB — I LIKE IT!

IT'S ALMOST TIME FOR YOUR FLEECING.
I'M SUPPOSED TO PREPARE YOU.
I HAVE TO DETERMINE HOW MANY SNIPS FLEECE WILL TAKE.
AND FOR THAT I MULTIPLY YOUR AGE BY MY AGE....

KNOCK KNOCK
DID YOU HEAR THAT?
MAYBE FLEECE IS EARLY.
I SAID I'D HYPNOTIZE YOU FIRST.
OH DEAR!
YOU'RE GETTING SLEEPY... SLEEPY...
WHO AM I FOOLING? SHE'S ALREADY SLEEPY.
I'M COMING!

WEEK TWELVE THE REPRESSED

DR. FLOYD
OH, IT'S YOU.
I KNOW I'M EARLY. CAN I COME IN?
DR. FLOYD
I'M HERE WITH SOMEONE.
THE WOLF IS AFTER ME!
HEY, WHO IS THAT?
SHE LOOKS FAMILIAR.
DR. FLOYD
HI, MOM.
SHE'S SLEEPING.
SHE LOOKS DRUNK.

KNOCK
FLEECE?
I'LL JUST SLIP UNDER HERE. O.K., MOM?

WHERE IS SHE?
DR. FLOYD
YOU'RE NOT FLEECE!
THIS DR. FLEECE — WHAT DO WE REALLY KNOW ABOUT HIM?
HE'S ON HIS WAY HERE.
DR. FLOYD
WHAT IF FLEECE IS IN IT JUST FOR THE WOOL?
DR
WHAT IF LAMBSKIN IS ALL WOOL?
THEN THERE WON'T BE ANYTHING LEFT FOR YOU TO MISS.
IS THAT MY LAMBSKIN OVER THERE?

I THINK I'LL GO OVER THERE FOR A SEC.
I'LL SAVE SOME WOOL FOR YOU.
I'M COMING, LAMBSKIN!
HELLO, LOVE.
OH DEAR.
KNOCK
TIME FOR OUR GET-AWAY!
FLEECE?
HELP!

WHERE IS MY WOOLY BATHMAT?
WE TALKED ABOUT THIS!
I'VE HAD SECOND THOUGHTS. DO YOU LIKE THESE GLASSES?
DR. FLOYD
FLOYD, I HAVE GIVEN YOU SO MUCH.
CRUMBS, IDEAS ... JEEZ ... I EVEN TOLD YOU ABOUT MY BURIED THINGS.
YOU WANTED TO.
NO, YOU MADE ME DIG THEM UP.
YOU MADE ME COME CLEAN.
AND ONCE I COME CLEAN...
I MUST COME DRY.

WELL, WELL, WHAT HAVE WE HERE?
COME ON, LAMBSKIN!
YOU SEE, SHE'S RESISTANT.
WHAT IS THIS?
WHO ARE YOU?
KNOCK
DID YOU HEAR THAT?
WHAT?
MOM?
FLEECE?

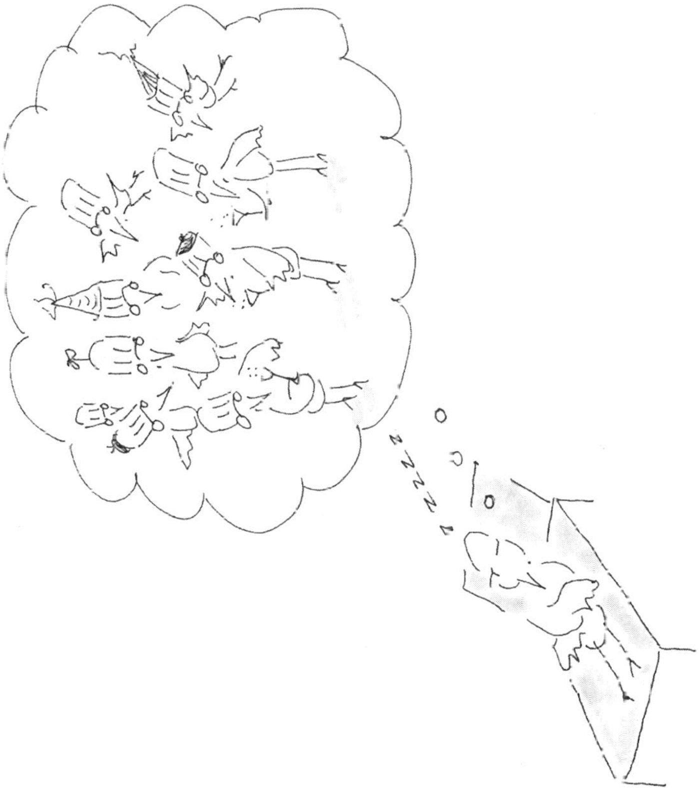

EVERYONE, OUT! OUT! OUT!
?
?
?
?
DR.
BOY! AM I TIRED!
A NAP.
OOF!
THERE.

SOFT!
VERY NICE!
I SHOULD DO THIS MORE OFTEN.
VERY RESTFUL.
I WONDER WHY I'M NOT ASLEEP.
GLASSES.
ZZZZZ

DR. FLOYD
COME ON!
COME ON!
HURRY!
DR.
ZZZZZ

ROLL IT TIGHTER!
ZZZZZZ
STUFF IT IN THERE!
ZZZZ
LET'S GO! WE GOT WHAT WE CAME FOR!
DR. LOYD

ZZZZZZ
HAVING A NICE TIME AT THE PARTY, DR. FLOYD?
LET'S TALK OVER HERE WHERE IT'S QUIET.
YOU LOOK AWFUL!
I FEEL SICK.
WHAT'S WRONG?
TERRIBLE STOMACH ACHE!

SAY AAHHH!
BAAHH!
SOMEONE HELP! SOMETHING IS WRONG!
ACHHH!
LET ME PERCUSS HER.
THAT'S NOT PERCUSSING.
OWWW!
THIS DIRTY SYRINGE OUGHTA HELP.
SNIP!

WHAT A DREAM!
IT WAS AWFUL!
LAMBSKIN LOOKED TERRIBLE.
WOLFMAN ALMOST SQUEEZED THE LIFE OUT OF HER.
I LOVE HER TO DEATH!
RATMA'AM'S INJECTION MADE THINGS WORSE.
BUNNYMAN ALMOST LOST HIS MOTHER AGAIN.

SO WHY DO I FEEL SO GOOD?
BECAUSE I WAS BLAME-LESS!
WHICH MEANS...
A DREAM IS THE FULFILLMENT OF A WISH.
WHERE'S LAMB-SKIN?
LAMBSKIN?!
KNOCK
IS THAT YOU, FLEECE?
THERE'S ONLY ONE ESCAPE BETTER THAN A DREAM.

DR. FLOYD

NOTES

p. iii: See *Freud: A Life for Our Time,* by Peter Gay (New York: W. W. Norton, 1988), p. 135. One hundred years ago, in 1901, Freud, buoyed after finishing *The Interpretation of Dreams* and his self-analysis, overcame a deep fear of visiting Rome and the Pantheon. As Peter Gay relates, on September 3, 1901, in a note dated "at noon, opposite the Pantheon," Freud wrote to his wife, "So this is what I had been afraid of for years!"

p. 3: *I am afraid of the wolf.* See "Analysis of a Phobia in a Five-Year-Old Boy" (Little Hans [1909]), in *Collected Papers,* by Sigmund Freud, edited by Ernest Jones (New York: Basic Books, 1959), Volume 3, translated by Alix and James Strachey, p. 165. Freud records Little Hans's father talking about the boy's phobia: "He is afraid that a horse will bite him in the street, and this fear seems somehow to be connected with his having been frightened by a large penis"—or, as Hans called it, a large "widdler."

p. 4: *You dirty swindler!* See *The Correspondence of Sigmund Freud and Sandor Ferenczi,* Volume I: 1908–1914, edited by Eva Brabant, Ernst Falzeder, and Patrizia Giampieri-Deutsch and translated by Peter T. Hoffer (Cambridge: Belknap/Harvard University Press, 1993), p. 138. On February 13, 1910, Freud wrote to Ferenczi about the Wolf Man after his first visit: "A rich young Russian, whom I took on because of compulsive tendencies, admitted the following transferences to me after the first session: Jewish swindler, he would like to use me from behind and shit on my head."

p. 6: *Tell me whatever pops into your head.* See "Notes Upon a Case of Obsessional Neurosis" (The Rat Man [1909]), in *Three Case Histories,* by Sigmund Freud, translated by Alix and James Strachey and edited by Philip Rieff (New York: Collier/Macmillan, 1963), p. 20. Freud wrote that he ordered the Rat Man to "pledge himself to submit to the one and only condition of the treatment—namely to say everything that came into his head."

p. 6: *You don't mind if I snack, do you?* See *Freud: A Life,* p. 266. "The Rat Man was something of a favorite with Freud from the beginning," Gay writes. "There is a cryptic entry in Freud's notes for December 28 [1907] that attests to his feelings for his patient: *Hungerig und wird gelabt*—'Hungry and is refreshed.' Freud had invited his patient to a meal. This was a heretical gesture for a psychoanalyst."

p. 7: *Let's talk about your bag of crumbs.* See *Three Case Histories,* p. 17. In the first few pages of the Rat Man case, Freud admitted he could only offer "crumbs of knowledge."

p. 19: *Your mother.* See *Collected Papers,* Volume 3, p. 253. Little Hans, Freud writes, "was really a little Oedipus who wanted to have his father 'out of the way,' to get rid of him, so that he might be alone with his handsome mother and sleep with her." And p. 224. As Freud noted, Hans told his father that he wanted him "to fall down," and then he elaborated on his fantasy: "You've got to be naked . . . and blood must flow, and then I'll be able to be alone with Mummy for a little bit at all events." See also p. 215. Hans's father scolded him for wanting his mother so badly. "A good boy doesn't wish that sort of thing." Little Hans replied: "But he may think it." And Freud applauded him in a footnote: "Well done, Little Hans! I could wish for no better understanding of psychoanalysis from a grown-up."

p. 21: *I just love tormenting little critters . . .* See "From the History of an Infantile Neurosis" (The Wolf Man [1918]), in *Three Case Histories,* p. 208–9. The Wolf Man was cruel to small animals. "As a result of the suppression of his onanism, the boy's sex life took on a sadistic-anal character. He became irritable and a tormentor, and gratified himself in this way at the expense of animals. . . . He began to be cruel to small animals, to catch flies and pull out their wings, to crush beetles underfoot; in his imagination he liked beating large animals (horses) as well."

p. 21: *My father, my sister, butterflies, pictures of wolves walking upright* . . . See *Three Case Histories,* p. 198. The Wolf Man, starting at age five, "had suffered from a fear, which his sister exploited for the purpose of tormenting him. There was a particular picture book, in which a wolf was represented standing upright and striding along. . . . Meanwhile, he was also frightened by other animals as well, big and little . . . a big beautiful butterfly . . . beetles and caterpillars. . . . Horses, too." He made these associations after telling Freud his famous dream. See also below, the second note for page 30 ("I am terrified . . .").

p. 21: *A certain dream* . . . See *Freud: A Life,* p. 288. Freud nicknamed the Wolf Man for his famous dream, a dream that, Gay writes, "stands second in the psychoanalytic literature only to . . . [Freud's own] historic dream of Irma's injection." See also below, the notes for page 30 for the Wolf Man's dream and the note for page 120 for Freud's dream of Irma's injection.

p. 22: *Your glasses, Dr. Floyd.* See *Three Case Histories,* pp. 26–28. The Rat Man's "great obsessive fear" centered on the return of money for some eyeglasses. When he was a soldier, he told Freud, he lost his pince-nez and wired his "opticians in Vienna to send . . . another pair." That evening he got a packet with the pince-nez that he had sent for. His captain handed him the packet, saying, "Lieutenant A. has paid the charges for you. You must pay him back."

p. 23: *If you don't take them, something awful will happen.* See *Three Case Histories,* pp. 27–28. The Rat Man was obsessed with contradictory thoughts: "that he was not to pay back the money" and that he "must pay back the 3.80 crowns to Lieutenant A." or else his girlfriend and his father would be subjected to a certain "punishment." See also below, the first note for page 83 (First, what is this "rat torture"?).

p. 24: *I keep hearing strange animals.* See "The Case of Frau Emmy Von N." (1889) in *Studies on Hysteria,* by Josef Breuer and Sigmund Freud, translated by James Strachey in collaboration with Anna Freud and assisted by Alix Strachey and Alan Tyson (New York: Basic Books, 1996), pp. 72–74 and p. 52. Emmy von N. suffered from zoopsia, or animal hallucinations, including visions of mice, horses, bulls, and worms. She told Freud that her zoopsia probably had to do with the fact that when she was five years old "my brothers and sisters often threw dead animals at me."

p. 30: [*Wolfman's tree*] See *Three Case Histories,* p. 214. In the case history of the Wolf Man, Freud published this reproduction of the Wolf Man's sketch of his childhood dream.

p. 30: *I am terrified to see a pack of wolves sitting in a tree . . .* See *Three Case Histories,* p. 213. Here is the text of the Wolf Man's dream: "I dreamt that it was night and that I was lying in my bed. . . . Suddenly the window opened of its own accord, and I was terrified to see that some white wolves were sitting on the big walnut tree in front of the window. There were six or seven of them. The wolves were quite white, and looked more like foxes or sheep-dogs, for they had big tails like foxes and they had their ears pricked like dogs when they are attending to something. In great terror, evidently of being eaten up by the wolves, I screamed and woke up."

p. 31: *They remind me of the sheep we used to visit . . .* See *Three Case Histories,* p. 215. When the Wolf Man thought about the white wolves in his dream, they "made him think of the sheep, large flocks of which were kept in the neighborhood of the estate. His father occasionally took him with him to visit these flocks, and every time this happened he felt very proud and blissful."

p. 31: *A fairy tale.* See *Three Case Histories,* p. 215. The Wolf Man's dream reminded him of a story his grandfather told him: "A tailor was sitting at work in his room, when the window opened and a wolf leapt in. The tailor . . . caught him by his tail and pulled it off, so that the wolf ran away in terror. Some time later the tailor went into the forest, and suddenly saw a pack of wolves coming towards him; so he climbed a tree to escape from them. At first the wolves were in perplexity; but the maimed one, which was among them and wanted to revenge himself upon the tailor, proposed they should climb one upon another till the last one could reach him . . . but the tailor recognized the visitor whom he had punished, and suddenly called out as he had before: 'Catch the grey one by his tail!' The tailless wolf, terrified by the recollection, ran away, and all the others tumbled down."

p. 31: *Castration anxiety!* See *Three Case Histories,* p. 216. Freud said the Wolf Man's dream "contains an unmistakable allusion to the castration complex."

p. 32: *Compulsive washing!* See "Obsessive Acts and Religious Practices" (1907) in *Collected Papers,* Volume 2, translated under the supervision of Joan Riviere. p. 26. In 1905, Freud found a similarity between neurotic rites and religious ceremonies. "The neurotic ceremonial consists of little prescriptions, restrictions and arrangements in certain activities of everyday life which have to be carried out always in the same or in a methodically varied way."

p. 34: *Sounds like hysteria! . . . First you hear strange animals, now you are a doormat.* See the general index to *Studies on Hysteria,* p. 329, which includes zoopsia (visions of animals) and paralysis as symptoms of hysteria.

p. 34: *Hypnosis?* See *Studies on Hysteria,* p. 256. Freud noted that he had tried out "Breuer's method of treating hysterical symptoms by an investigation and abreaction of them under hypnosis."

p. 35: *Father would pay a small price . . . me.* See *Dora: An Analysis of a Case of Hysteria* (1905), by Sigmund Freud, edited by Philip Rieff (New York: Collier/Macmillan, 1963), pp. 50–51. Dora's father was having an affair with a women named Frau K., and so he looked the other way when Frau K.'s husband, Herr K., tried to seduce Dora. Dora, Freud wrote, was "overcome by the idea that she had been handed over to Herr K. as the price of his tolerating the relations between her father and his wife." And p. 80: "She had been sacrificed by her father."

p. 38: *I can see you as long as you can pay.* See *Freud: A Life,* p. 297. Gay writes that Freud expected "that the cultivated men and women visiting his consulting room will 'treat matters of money as they do matters of sex, with the same inconsistency, prudishness, hypocrisy.' " To avoid confusion and to insure regular payment, Freud suggested the following plan: "The patient agrees to lease a certain hour of the analyst's time and pays for it whether he avails himself of it or not."

p. 41: *Their silence is great commotion.* See *Three Case Histories,* pp. 222–23. Freud famously interpreted the silence of the wolves in the Wolf Man's dream as proof that when the Wolf Man was a year and a half old he saw his parents having sex. It was "in the afternoon, possibly at five o'clock . . . [on] a hot summer's day . . . [and] his parents had retired, half undressed, for an afternoon *siesta.* When he woke up, he witnessed a coitus *a tergo* [from behind], three times repeated; he was able to see his mother's genitals as well as his father's member."

p. 41: *I take your protest for agreement.* See below, the second note for page 84 (" 'No' means 'yes' ").

p. 43: *I was a sneaky, sniveling little spy as a child.* See *Three Case Histories,* p. 23. When he was a child, the Rat Man "was under the domination of a component of the sexual instinct, scoptophilia (the instinct of looking)," Freud wrote.

p. 44: *Did I tell you how one of them pounced on me?* See *Dora,* pp. 41–43. When she was sixteen years old, Dora "told her mother—intending that what she said should be passed on to her father—that Herr K. had had the audacity to make her a proposal while they were on a walk after a trip upon the lake." Two years earlier, when Dora was fourteen years old, Herr K. had made arrangements to be alone with her and "suddenly clasped the girl to him and pressed a kiss upon her lips."

p. 44: *Cough! Cough!* See *Dora,* pp. 36–37. At age twelve, Dora "began to suffer . . . from attacks of nervous coughing." At age sixteen, when Freud first saw her, "she was suffering from a cough and from hoarseness." At age eighteen, when she came to Freud for treatment again, "she was again coughing in a characteristic manner" and suffered "a complete loss of voice."

p. 44: *It was horrible.* See *Dora,* p. 43. When Dora was forcibly kissed by Herr K., which Freud described as "surely just the situation to call up a distinct feeling of sexual excitement in a girl of fourteen," she "had at that moment a violent feeling of disgust." See also p. 45. Freud guessed "that during the man's passionate embrace she felt not merely his kiss upon her lips but also the pressure of his erect member against her body. This perception was revolting to her."

p. 45: *No, just a tickle.* See *Dora,* p. 68. Freud wrote, "it is not to be wondered at that this hysterical girl of nineteen, who had heard of the occurrence of such a method of sexual intercourse (sucking at the male organ), should have developed an unconscious phantasy of this sort and should have given it expression by an irritation in her throat and by coughing." And p. 65, where Freud wrote: "The conclusion was inevitable that with her spasmodic cough, which, as is usual, was referred for its exciting cause to a tickling in her throat, she pictured to herself a scene of sexual gratification *per os* [by mouth] between the two people whose love-affair occupied her mind so incessantly, her father and Frau K."

p. 45: *You're in love with the old wolf.* See *Dora,* p. 55. Freud wrote that Dora's "illness was a demonstration of her love for K."

p. 45: *I slapped him!* See *Dora,* p. 63. When Herr K. made Dora a proposal by the lake, "She had given him a slap in the face and hurried away."

p. 51: *Would he love me? Or would he kill me?* See *Three Case Histories,* p. 228. Freud interpreted the Wolf Man's dream as "a reflection of the progress of the dreamer's thoughts during the construction of the dream: 'longing for sexual satisfaction from his father—realization that castration is a necessary condition of it—fear of his father.' "

p. 51: *You know, Lambskin barely has a tail.* See *Three Case Histories,* p. 234. Freud saw the Wolf Man's fear of castration in the dream as an aspect of his sexual identification with his mother. "It seems, therefore, as though he had identified himself with his castrated mother during the dream, and was now fighting against that fact. 'If you want to be sexually satisfied by Father,' we may perhaps represent him as saying to himself, 'you must allow yourself to be castrated like Mother, but I won't have that.' In short, a clear protest on the part of his masculinity!"

p. 52: *And I've preserved them by burying them.* See *Three Case Histories,* p. 36. To explain to the Rat Man why digging up unpleasant unconscious ideas helps destroy them, Freud used the analogy of burial: "I explained that . . . everything conscious was subject to a process of wearing–away, while what was unconscious was relatively unchangeable; and I illustrated my remarks by pointing to the antiques standing about in my room. . . . Their burial had been their preservation: the destruction of Pompeii was only beginning now that it had been dug up."

p. 53: *I liked to peek up skirts.* See *Three Case Histories,* p. 21. "My sexual life began very early," the Rat Man informed Freud. "We had a very pretty young governess called Fräulein Peter. . . . I was lying beside her, and begged her to let me creep under her skirt. She told me I might, so long as I said nothing to any one about it." See above, the note for page 43 ("I was a sneaky . . . child").

p. 54: *A fire.* See *Dora,* p. 81. Here is the dream as related by Dora: "A house was on fire. My father was standing beside my bed and woke me up. I dressed myself quickly. Mother wanted to stop and save her jewel-case; but Father said: 'I refuse to let myself and my two children be burnt for the sake of your jewel-case.' " Dora "remembered having had the dream three nights in succession" at the lake, where Herr K. proposed to her, Freud wrote. See also above, the first note for page 44 ("Did I tell you . . . ?").

p. 55: *Psst . . . It's a jewel case.* See *Dora,* pp. 94–95. One day Dora wore "a small reticule . . . and, as she lay on the sofa and talked, she kept playing with it—opening it, putting a finger into it, shutting it again, and so on." Freud wrote that this "was an entirely unembarrassed yet unmistakable pantomimic announcement of what she would like to do with them [her hands]—namely to masturbate." And p. 87. Freud also told Dora "that 'jewel-case' [schmuck-kästchen] is a favorite expression . . . for the female genitals."

p. 59: *Your jealous father?* See *Collected Papers,* Volume 3, p. 253. Freud interpreted Little Hans's fear of horses as an Oedipal fear. It sprang from his "death-wish against his father."

p. 60: *I go to her and say, "Lamb-god."* See *Three Case Histories,* p. 199. When the Wolf Man was a child, "he was very pious. . . . He was obliged to think 'God—swine' or 'God—shit.' . . . Once while he was on a journey to a health-resort in Germany he was tormented by the obsession of having to think of the Holy Trinity whenever he saw three heaps of horse-dung or other excrement lying in the road."

p. 62: *Lamp! Towel! Plate!* See *Three Case Histories,* pp. 62–63. As a youth, when the Rat Man was caught doing "something naughty . . . his father had given him a beating. The boy had flown into a terrible rage. . . . But as he knew no bad language, he . . . had screamed, 'You lamp! You towel! You plate!' and so on. His father, shaken by the outburst, had stopped beating him, and had declared: 'The child will be either a great man or a great criminal!' "

p. 63: *If only my family would die tragically.* See *Three Case Histories,* p. 38. The idea occurred to the Rat Man "that his father's death might make him rich enough to marry" his girlfriend. And p. 37. This fantasy was connected with an earlier one: "When he was twelve years old, he had been in love with a little girl . . . [and] the idea had come to him that she would be kind to him if some misfortune were to befall him."

p. 63: *I could kill for this!* See *Three Case Histories,* p. 59. Freud noted that the first time the Rat Man had sex, which was several years after the death of his father, "an idea sprang into his mind: 'This is glorious! One might murder one's father for this!' "

p. 65: *You know what they say about shells?* See *A General Introduction to Psychoanalysis,* by Sigmund Freud, translated by Joan Riviere (Garden City, N.Y.: Garden City Publishing Co., 1943), p. 139. "From the animal world, snails and mussels at any rate must be cited as unmistakable female symbols." See also above, the note for page 55 ("Psst . . .").

p. 69: *My brothers and sisters told me we came from . . . you know . . . like . . . dung.* See *Collected Papers,* Volume 3, p. 211 (note 1) and p. 208. Little Hans talked about his sister Hanna right after speaking about "lumfs" (pieces of dung). Freud noted: "and the explanation of this . . . begins to dawn upon us: Hanna was a lumf herself—babies were lumfs."

p. 71: *No. I just miss that soft skin.* See "Psychoanalytic Notes Upon an Autobiographical Account of a Case of Paranoia" (Dementia Paranoides—Dr. Schreber, 1911) in *Three Case Histories,* p. 129. Mr. Wolfman shares some features not just with the Wolf Man, who sexually identified with his mother, but also with Daniel Paul Schreber, a prominent judge who suffered paranoid delusions and wrote a memoir about them, which Freud analyzed. Among other delusions, Schreber "felt that he was God's wife" and thought that his nerves had "given to his body a more or less female stamp, and more particularly to his skin a softness peculiar to the female sex."

p. 71: *It's my father who would pounce.* See *Three Case Histories,* p. 274. Freud noted that the Wolf Man had "precisely the same impulse towards God which was expressed in unambiguous words in the delusional system of the paranoic Senatspräsident Schreber." He was ready to give up his masculinity if he could "be loved like a woman." See below, the second note for p. 81 ("God-the-Father . . .").

p. 73: *Something . . . called the "rat torture."* See *Three Case Histories,* p. 26. Shortly after the Rat Man lost his glasses and wired his optician to send another pair, he fell into conversation with an army captain. The Rat Man told Freud about the event: "The Captain told me he had read of a specially horrible punishment used in the East. . . ." See also below, the first note for page 83 ("First, what is this rat torture?").

p. 73: *If I don't pay you back, then someone will face the "rat torture."* See *Three Case Histories,* pp. 27–28. After the Rat Man told Freud about the horrible punishment, he said, "At that moment the idea flashed through my mind that this was happening to a person who was very dear to me," the Rat Man's girlfriend. Then, Freud added, The Rat Man was "obliged to admit that a second idea had occurred to him simultaneously, namely, the idea of the punishment also being applied to his father."

p. 74: *I bet she loves me, too.* See *Dora,* p. 92. After Freud analyzed Dora's fire dream and connected it with the smoking habits not only of Herr K. and her father but also his own, he noted, "I came to the conclusion that the idea had probably occurred to her one day during a sitting that she would like to have a kiss from me."

p. 75: *I love my father, but he is insincere, false, and selfish.* See *Dora,* p. 50. Freud noted that Dora, who was enraged at her father for sacrificing her welfare in order to carry on his romantic affair (see above, the note for page 35), listed her criticisms of her father: "he was insincere, he had a strain of falseness in his character, he thought only of his own enjoyment, and he had a gift for seeing things in the light which suited him best."

p. 75: *I've suckled a few in my day.* See *Dora,* p. 53. When it came to Herr K.'s children, Dora "had been a mother to them, she had taught them, she had gone for walks with them, she had offered them a complete substitute for the slight interest which their own mother showed in them."

p. 75: *Their mother was always—ahem!—sick* See *Dora,* p. 55. Dora had "learned from observing Frau K. [her father's mistress] what useful things illnesses could become," Freud noted. He then asked, "Could it be that the presence or absence of the man she [Dora] loved had had an influence upon the appearance and disappearance of the symptoms of her illness?"

p. 80: *I have to hold my breath . . . or I might become weak like her.* See *Three Case Histories,* p. 199. The Wolf Man used to carry out a "peculiar ceremonial when he saw people that he felt sorry for, such as beggars, cripples, or very old men. He had to breathe out noisily, so as not to become like them."

p. 81: *I think he'd even kill his own son.* See *Three Case Histories,* pp. 253–54. The Wolf Man's masochistic attitude toward his father led to an identification: "He became Christ." But "he also rebelled against the passive character of Christ and against his ill-treatment by his father, and in this way began also to renounce his previous masochistic ideal, even in its sublimation." He noted that "God had treated his son harshly and cruelly, but he was no better toward men; he had sacrificed his own son and had ordered Abraham to do the same."

p. 81: *God-the-Father. He thinks I'm his plaything.* See *Three Case Histories,* p. 253. At the same time that the Wolf Man was voicing hostility toward God, his own identification with Christ was undergoing a change. He began "doubting whether Christ could have a behind . . . whether he himself could be used by his father like a woman." See also above, the notes for page 71.

p. 83: *First, what is this "rat torture"?* See *Three Case Histories,* pp. 26–27. After getting up from the sofa and begging Freud to spare him from having to recite the details, the Rat Man described the rat torture: "The criminal was tied up . . . a pot was turned upside down on his buttocks . . . some rats were put into it . . . and they . . . bored their way in . . ." Freud then completed the sentence, which the Rat Man himself was unable to do: "Into his anus."

p. 83: *Father . . . Boyfriend.* See above, the note for page 23 and the second note for page 73 ("If I don't pay you . . .").

p. 84: *Which proves that you're in love with Mr. Wolfman.* See *Dora,* p. 53. Freud interpreted Dora's preoccupation with Herr K.'s children as "a bond between Herr K. and Dora" and a sign "that she had all these years been in love with Herr K."

p. 84: *"No" means "yes."* See *Dora,* pp. 75–76. Freud wrote famously about Dora's emphatic denials of being in love with Herr K., Frau K., and her father: "There is no such thing as an unconscious 'No.' " The word acts "as a gauge of the repression's strength. . . . 'No' signifies the desired 'yes.' "

p. 85: *This is a talking cure, you know.* See *Studies on Hysteria,* p. 30. It was Anna O., a patient of Freud's colleague and mentor Josef Breuer, who came up with the term "talking cure." She also called it "chimney-sweeping."

p. 85: *I think I'd better consult Dr. Fleece.* See *Freud: A Life,* pp. 55–57. While Freud was treating Dora, he was corresponding with his friend Wilhelm Fliess, an ear, nose, and throat doctor. Fliess had some "fanciful notions" about treatment, Gay writes, including the "proposition that one organ casts its shadow over the others" and, in particular, that nose surgery could cure sexual or genital disorders.

p. 88: *I call it "Little dung or little child?"* See *Collected Papers,* Volume 3, p. 217. Little Hans made a comparison between a piece of dung (a "lumf") and a baby, concluding that "A lumf's much bigger." Freud wrote: "I had predicted to his father that it would be possible to trace back Hans's phobia to thoughts and wishes occasioned by the birth of his baby sister. But I had omitted to point out that according to the sexual theory of children a baby is a 'lumf' so that Hans's path would lie through the excremental complex." See also above, the note for page 69.

p. 88: *Then I crawl underneath.* See *Collected Papers,* Volume 3, p. 253. At age five, Little Hans's most important pleasure was "that of sleeping beside his mother," his father told Freud.

p. 89: *I kind of prefer the idea of storks with bundles.* See *Collected Papers,* Volume 3, p. 216. Despite Hans's many creative ideas about where babies come from, he did not buy the stork story. "A stork can't do it," he said.

p. 91: *The fleecing of the lamb!* See *The Complete Letters of Sigmund Freud to Wilhelm Fliess, 1887–1904,* edited and translated by Jeffrey Moussaieff Masson (Cambridge: Belknap/Harvard University Press, 1985), pp. 116–17. Freud allowed Fliess to perform nose surgery on his patient Emma Eckstein. The surgery did not turn out well: some gauze was accidentally left in her nose and as a result she suffered serious hemorrhaging. Freud wrote Fliess a letter describing Eckstein's condition two weeks after surgery: "I asked Rosanes [another surgeon] to meet me. . . . There still was moderate bleeding from the nose and mouth; the fetid odor was very bad. Rosanes cleaned the area surrounding the opening, removed some sticky blood clots, and suddenly pulled at something like a thread, kept on pulling. Before either of us had time to think, at least half a meter of gauze had been removed from the cavity. The next moment came a flood of blood. The patient turned white, her eyes bulged, and she had no pulse. . . . It lasted about half a minute, but this was enough to make the poor creature, whom by then we had lying flat, unrecognizable. . . . So we had done her an injustice; she was not at all abnormal {i.e., the bleeding was not hysterical}, rather, a piece of iodoform gauze had gotten torn off as you were removing it and stayed in for fourteen days, preventing healing; at the end it tore off and provoked the bleeding." This horrific event came to haunt Freud's dreams.

p. 92: *It's Oedipal, stupid!* See *Three Case Histories,* p. 59. Freud wrote of the Rat Man, "There can be no question that there was something in the sphere of sexuality that stood between the father and son, and that the father had come into some sort of opposition to the son's prematurely developed erotic life."

p. 93: *If your father is dead, he can't suffer the "rat torture."* See *Three Case Histories,* p. 28. Freud pointed out that the Rat Man was obsessed with the idea that the rat punishment "would be applied to his father" even though "his father had died many years previously." And p. 38. Freud believed the Rat Man's guilt about the rat torture had to do with his fantasy that losing his father would make him attractive to women. See also above, the notes for pages 63 and 83.

p. 94: *Dr. Fleece has agreed to fleece you.* See above, the note for page 91.

p. 100: *Your feminine side.* See *Complete Letters of Sigmund Freud to Wilhelm Fliess,* p. 2. Jeffrey Masson writes in his introduction that both Freud and Fliess "believed that elements of bisexuality are inherent in all individuals."

p. 104: *And for that I multiply your age by my age . . .* See *Freud: A Life,* p. 56. "Fliess is now regarded as a crank and pathological numerologist," writes Gay. For example, he was "enslaved to a scheme of biorhythmic cycles of 23 and 28 days, to which males and females were seen to be subject and which, he believed, would permit the physician to diagnose all sorts of conditions and ailments."

p. 105: *You're getting sleepy . . . sleepy . . .* See *Freud: A Life,* p. 71. As Freud told his daughter Anna, he began to learn from his hysterical patients—particularly Emmy Von N.—that treatment by "hypnosis is a senseless and worthless proceeding." Learning this was crucial, Gay notes, for it forced him to create what Freud called "the more sensible psychoanalytic therapy."

p. 120: *zzzzz.* See *The Interpretation of Dreams,* by Sigmund Freud, translated and edited by James Strachey (New York: Avon Books, 1965), pp. 139–40. Freud's dream of Irma's injection was triggered by a memory of Fliess's botched nose surgery on Emma Eckstein. (See above, the note for page 91.) This was the dream: "A large hall—numerous guests, whom we were receiving—Among them was Irma. I at once took her on one side, as though to answer her letter and to reproach her for not having accepted my 'solution' yet. I said to her: 'If you still get pains, it's really only your fault.' She replied: 'If you only knew what pains I've got now in my throat and stomach and abdomen—it's choking me'—I was alarmed and looked at her. She looked pale and puffy. I thought to myself that after all I must be missing some organic trouble. I took her to the window and looked down her throat, and she showed signs of recalcitrance, like women with artificial dentures. I thought to myself that there was really no need for her to do that.—She then opened her mouth properly and on the right I found a big white patch; at another place I saw extensive whitish grey scabs upon some remarkable curly structures which were evidently modelled on the turbinal bones of the nose.—I at once called in Dr. M., and he repeated the examination and confirmed it. . . . Dr. M. looked quite different from usual; he was very pale, he walked with a limp and his chin was clean-shaven. . . . My friend Otto was now standing beside her as well, and my friend Leopold was percussing her through her bodice and saying: 'She has a dull area low down on the left.' He also indicated that a portion of the skin on the left shoulder was infiltrated. (I noticed this, just as he did, in spite of her dress.) . . . M. said: "There's no doubt it's an infection, but no matter; dysentery will supervene and the toxin will be eliminated.' . . . We were directly aware, too, of the origin of her infection. Not long before, when she was feeling unwell, my friend Otto had given her an injection of a preparation of propyl, propyls . . . propionic acid . . . trimethylamin (and I saw before me the formula for this printed in heavy type). . . . Injections of that sort ought not to be made so thoughtlessly. . . . And probably the syringe had not been clean."

p. 123: *Because I was blameless!* See *The Interpretation of Dreams,* p. 151. Freud wrote, "The dream acquitted me of the responsibility for Irma's condition by showing that it was due to other factors—it produced a whole series of reasons. The dream represented a particular state of affairs as I should have wished it to be. Thus its content was the fulfillment of a wish and its motive was a wish."

p. 123: *A dream is the fulfillment of a wish.* See *Freud: A Life,* pp. 80–82. Freud was thrilled with his interpretation of his dream of Irma's injection. As Gay writes: "Freud gave it exceptional stature, using it as a paradigm for his theory that dreams are wish fulfillments." Freud even predicted that some day at Bellevue, the resort villa near Vienna where he had had the dream, there would be a marble plaque reading: "Here revealed itself, on July 29, 1895, the secret of the dream to Dr. Sigm. Freud."

ACKNOWLEDGMENTS

I would like to thank the two people who kept me more or less sane while I was working on *In the Floyd Archives:* my sister, Susan Boxer, a psychologist with a poet's ear and no resemblance to Dr. Floyd, and Harry Cooper, my husband, reader, special-effects man, and in-house optimist.

ABOUT THE AUTHOR

Sarah Boxer was born in Denver, Colorado, and earned her B.A. in philosophy at Harvard. She is a critic and reporter at the *New York Times,* where she writes about photography, psychoanalysis, art, animals, philosophy, and other subjects. At the age of eleven she published her first cartoon, and at fifteen she began reading Freud. She lives with her husband in New York City and Cambridge, Massachusetts.